The Wit and Wisdom

Wisdom

Bruce Lee

Peter Jennings

D1470406

For Kali

"I'm not in this world to live up to your expectations and you're not in this world to live up to mine."

— Bruce Lee

"Do not pray for an easy life, pray for the strength to endure a difficult one"

— Bruce Lee

"Be like water making its way through cracks. Do not be assertive, but adjust to the object, and you shall find a way around or through it. If nothing within you stays rigid, outward things will disclose themselves.

Empty your mind, be formless. Shapeless, like water. If you put water into a cup, it becomes the cup. You put water into a bottle and it becomes the bottle. You put it in a teapot, it becomes the teapot. Now, water can flow or it can crash. Be water, my friend."

— Bruce Lee

"Be happy, but never satisfied."

— Bruce Lee

"Adapt what is useful, reject what is useless, and add what is specifically your own."

— Bruce Lee

"Mistakes are always forgivable, if one has the courage to admit them."

— Bruce Lee

"Love is like a friendship caught on fire. In the beginning a flame, very pretty, often hot and fierce, but still only light and flickering. As love grows older, our hearts mature and our love becomes as coals, deep-burning and unquenchable."

— Bruce Lee

"A wise man can learn more from a foolish question than a fool can learn from a wise answer."

— Bruce Lee

"If you always put limits on everything you do, physical or anything else, it will spread into your work and into your life. There are no limits. There are only plateaus, and you must not stay there, you must go beyond them."

— Bruce Lee

"I fear not the man who has practiced 10,000 kicks once, but I fear the man who had practiced one kick 10,000 times."

— Bruce Lee

"If you spend too much time thinking about a thing, you'll never get it done."

— Bruce Lee

"Don't fear failure. — Not failure, but low aim, is the crime. In great attempts it is glorious even to fail."

— Bruce Lee, Bruce Lee Striking

"A goal is not always meant to be reached, it often serves simply as something to aim at."

— Bruce Lee

"To hell with circumstances; I create opportunities."

— Bruce Lee

"The doubters said,

"Man can not fly,"

The doers said,

"Maybe, but we'll try,"

And finally soared

In the morning glow

While non-believers

Watched from below."

— Bruce Lee

"The key to immortality is first living a life worth remembering."

— Bruce Lee

"Knowing is not enough, we must apply. Willing is not enough, we must do."

— Bruce Lee

"If you don't want to slip up tomorrow, speak the truth today."

— Bruce Lee

"It is not a daily increase, but a daily decrease. Hack away at the inessentials."

— Bruce Lee

"Use only that which works, and take it from any place you can find it."

— Bruce Lee, Tao of Jeet Kune Do

"Always be yourself, express yourself, have faith in yourself, do not go out and look for a successfull personality and duplicate it."

— Bruce Lee

"Not being tense but ready.

Not thinking but not dreaming.

Not being set but flexible.

Liberation from the uneasy sense of confinement.

It is being wholly and quietly alive, aware and alert, ready for whatever may come."

— Bruce Lee, Tao of Jeet Kune Do

"A quick temper will make a fool of you soon enough."

— Bruce Lee

"Notice that the stiffest tree is most easily cracked, while the bamboo or willow survives by bending with the wind."

— Bruce Lee

"Empty your cup so that it may be filled; become devoid to gain totality."

— Bruce Lee

"The great mistake is to anticipate the outcome of the engagement; you ought not to be thinking of whether it ends in victory or defeat. Let nature take its course, and your tools will strike at the right moment."

— Bruce Lee

"Forget about winning and losing; forget about pride and pain. Let your opponent graze your skin and you smash into his flesh; let him smash into your flesh and you fracture his bones; let him fracture your bones and you take his life! Do not be concerned with escaping safely- lay your life before him!!"

— Bruce Lee

"If there is a God, he is within. You don't ask God to give you things, you depend on God for your inner theme."

— Bruce Lee

"A good teacher protects his pupils from his own influence."

— Bruce Lee

"For it is easy to criticize and break down the spirit of others, but to know yourself takes a lifetime."

— Bruce Lee, Bruce Lee Striking Thoughts: Bruce Lee's Wisdom for Daily Living

"If you love life, don't waste time, for time is what life is made up of."

— Bruce Lee

"As you think, so shall you become."

— Bruce Lee

"To spend time is to pass it in a specified manner. To waste time is to expend it thoughtlessly or carelessly. We all have time to either spend or waste and it is our decision what to do with it. But once passed, it is gone forever."

— Bruce Lee

"Self-knowledge involves relationship. To know oneself is to study one self in action with another person. Relationship is a process of self evaluation and self revelation. Relationship is the mirror in which you discover yourself - to be is to be related."

— Bruce Lee

"Take things as they are. Punch when you have to punch. Kick when you have to kick."

— Bruce Lee

"Be self aware, rather than a repetitious robot"

— Bruce Lee

"Now I see that I will never find the light

Unless, like the candle, I am my own fuel,

Consuming myself."

— Bruce Lee

"Using no way as a way, having no limitation as limitation."

— Bruce Lee, Tao of Jeet Kune Do

"Many people dedicate their lives to actualizing a concept of what they should be like, rather than actualizing themselves.

This difference between self-actualization and self-image actualization is very important. Most people live only for their image"

— Bruce Lee

"Time means a lot to me because you see I am also a learner and am often lost in the joy of forever developing."

— Bruce Lee

"The spirit of the individual is determined by his dominating thought habits."

— Bruce Lee, Bruce Lee Jeet Kune Do: Bruce Lee's Commentaries on the Martial Way

"Defeat is not defeat unless accepted as a reality-in your own mind."

— Bruce Lee

"Art calls for complete mastery of techniques, developed by reflection within the soul."

— Bruce Lee

"Knowledge will give you power, but character respect."

— Bruce Lee

"Showing off is the fool's idea of glory."

— Bruce Lee

"The meaning of life is that it is to be lived, and it is not to be traded and conceptualized and squeezed into a patter of systems."

— Bruce Lee, Striking Thoughts: Bruce Lee's Wisdom for Daily Living

"The More we value things, the less we value ourselves"

— Bruce Lee

"Don't get set into one form, adapt it and build your own, and let it grow, be like water."

— Bruce Lee

"The stillness in stillness is not the real stillness; only when there is stillness in movement does the universal rhythm manifest."

— Bruce Lee

"Ever since I was a child I have had this instinctive urge for expansion and growth. To me, the function and duty of a quality human being is the sincere and honest development of one's potential."

— Bruce Lee

"Boards don't hit back."

— Bruce Lee

"Life's battles don't always go to the stronger or faster man. But sooner or later the man who wins, is the man who thinks he can."

— Bruce Lee

"Those who are unaware they are walking in darkness will never seek the light."

— Bruce Lee

"Everything you do, if not in a relaxed state will be done at a lesser level than you are proficient. Thus the tensed expert marksman will aim at a level less than his/her student."

— Bruce Lee

"Real living is living for others."

— Bruce Lee

"All knowledge leads to self-knowledge."

— Bruce Lee, Tao of Jeet Kune Do

"If nothing within you stays rigid, outward things will disclose themselves. Moving, be like water. Still, be like a mirror. Respond like an echo. "

— Bruce Lee

"The successful warrior is the average man, with laser-like focus."

— Bruce Lee

"Obey the principles without being bound by them."

— Bruce Lee

"Do not deny the classical approach, simply as a reaction, or you will have created another pattern and trapped yourself there."

— Bruce Lee, Tao of Jeet Kune Do

"To know oneself is to study oneself in action with another person."

"The idea is that flowing water never goes stale, so just keep on flowing."

— Bruce Lee

"It's like a finger pointing away to the moon. Don't concentrate on the finger or you will miss all that heavenly glory."

— Bruce Lee, Bruce Lee Striking Thoughts: Bruce Lee's Wisdom for Daily Living

"Preparation for tomorrow is hard work today."

— Bruce Lee

"The less effort, the faster and more powerful you will be."

— Bruce Lee

"You cannot force the Now. — But can you neither condemn nor justify and yet be extraordinarily alive as you walk on? You can never invite the wind, but you must leave the window open."

— Bruce Lee, Bruce Lee Striking Thoughts: Bruce Lee's Wisdom for Daily Living

"If you think a thing is impossible, you'll only make it impossible."

— Bruce Lee, Tao of Jeet Kune Do

"The world is full of people who are determined to be somebody or to give trouble. They want to get ahead, to stand out. Such ambition has no use for a kung fu man, who rejects all forms of self-assertiveness and competition"

— Bruce Lee, Bruce Lee Striking Thoughts: Bruce Lee's Wisdom for Daily Living

"The possession of anything begins in the mind."

— Bruce Lee

"...if you always put limits on what you can do, physical or anything else, it'll spread over into the rest of your life. It'll spread into your work, into your morality, into your entire being. There are no limits. There are plateaus, but you must not stay there, you must go beyond them. If it kills you, it kills you. A man must constantly exceed his level."

— Bruce Lee

"Linda and I aren't one and one. We are two halves that make a whole -- two halves fitted together are more efficient than either half would ever be alone!"

— Bruce Lee

"To me, the extraordinary aspect of martial arts lies in its simplicity. The easy way is also the right way, and martial arts is nothing at all special; the closer to the true way of martial arts, the less wastage of expression there is."

— Bruce Lee

"In Buddhism, there is no place for using effort. Just be ordinary and nothing special. Eat your food, move your bowels, pass water and when you're tired go and lie down. The ignorant will laugh at me, but the wise will understand."

— Bruce Lee, Tao of Jeet Kune Do

"It is compassion rather than the principle of justice which can guard us against being unjust to our fellow men."

— Bruce Lee, Tao of Jeet Kune Do

"Take no thought of who is right or wrong or who is better than. Be not for or against."

— Bruce Lee

"Knowledge earns you power, character earns you respect."

— Bruce Lee

"The word "superstar" is an illusion"

— Bruce Lee

"If I tell you I'm good, probably you will say I'm boasting. But if I tell you I'm not good, you'll know I'm lying."

— Bruce Lee

"All fixed set patterns are incapable of adaptability or pliability. The truth is outside of all fixed patterns."

— Bruce Lee

"As long as I can remember I feel I have had this great creative and spiritual force within me that is greater than faith, greater than ambition, greater than confidence, greater than determination, greater than vision. It is all these combined. My brain becomes magnetized with this dominating force which I hold in my hand."

— Bruce Lee

"Don't think. FEEL. It's like a finger pointing at the moon. Do not concentrate on the finger, or you will miss all of the heavenly glory."

— Bruce Lee

"Man, the living creature, the creating individual, is always more important than any established style or system."

— Bruce Lee

"Water is fearless, you put water into a cup, it becomes the cup, you put water into a teapot it becomes the teapot, water can flow drip, creep, or crash!"

— Bruce Lee

"The consciousness of self is the greatest hindrance to the proper execution of all physical action."

— Bruce Lee

"Set patterns, incapable of adaptability, of pliability, only offer a better cage. Truth is outside of all patterns."

— Bruce Lee, Tao of Jeet Kune Do

"Because one does not want to be disturbed, to be made uncertain, he establishes a pattern of conduct, of thought, a pattern of relationship to man etc. Then he becomes a slave to the patter and takes the pattern to be the real thing."

— Bruce Lee

"...we have more faith in what we imitate than in what we originate. We cannot derive a sense of absolute certitude from anything which has its roots in us. The most poignant sense of insecurity comes from standing alone and we are not alone when we imitate. It is thus with most of us; we are what other people say we are. We know ourselves chiefly by hearsay."

— Bruce Lee, Tao of Jeet Kune Do

"You just wait. I'm going to be the biggest Chinese Star in the world."

— Bruce Lee

"If you follow the classical pattern, you are understanding the routine, the tradition, the shadow -- you are not understanding yourself."

— Bruce Lee, Tao of Jeet Kune Do

"Bring the mind into sharp focus and make it alert so that it can immediately intuit truth, which is everywhere. The mind must be emancipated from old habits, prejudices, restrictive thought processes and even ordinary thought itself."

— Bruce Lee, Tao of Jeet Kune Do

"Using no way as way. Having no limitation as your only limitation."

— Bruce Lee, Tao of Jeet Kune Do

"Effort within the mind further limits the mind, because effort implies struggle towards a goal and when you have a goal, a purpose, an end in view, you have placed a limit on the mind."

— Bruce Lee, Tao of Jeet Kune Do

"The man who is really serious, with the urge to find out what truth is, has no style at all. He lives only in what is."

— Bruce Lee

"In order to control myself I must first accept myself by going with and not against my nature."

— Bruce Lee

"I'm moving and not moving at all. I'm like the moon underneath the waves that ever go on rolling and rocking. It is not, "I am doing this," but rather, an inner realization that "this is happening through me," or "it is doing this for me." The consciousness of self is the greatest hindrance to the proper execution of all physical action."

— Bruce Lee, Tao of Jeet Kune Do

"Having totality means being capable of following "what is," because "what is" is constantly moving and constantly changing. If one is anchored to a particular view, one will not be able to follow the swift movement of "what is."

— Bruce Lee, Tao of Jeet Kune Do

"There is no mystery about my style. My movements are simple, direct and non-classical. The extraordinary part of it lies in its simplicity. Every movement in Jeet Kune-Do is being so of itself. There is nothing artificial about it. I always believe that the easy way is the right way."

— Bruce Lee, Tao of Jeet Kune Do

"Voidness is that which stands right in the middle between this and that. The void is all-inclusive, having no opposite--there is nothing which it excludes or opposes. It is living void, because all forms come out of it and whoever realizes the void is filled with life and power and the love of all beings."

— Bruce Lee, Tao of Jeet Kune Do

"In the middle of chaos lies opportunity."

— Bruce Lee

"Only the self-sufficient stand alone - most people follow the crowd and imitate."

— Bruce Lee

"...good technique includes quick changes, great variety and speed. It may be a system of reversals much like a concept of God and the Devil. In the speed of events, which one is really in charge?...to put the heart of martial arts in your own heart and have it be a part of you means total comprehension and the use of a free style. When you have that you will know that there are no limits."

— Bruce Lee, Tao of Jeet Kune Do

"Remember no man is really defeated unless he is discouraged."

— Bruce Lee

"Satori - in the awakening from a dream. Awakening and self-realization and seeing into one's own being - these are synonymous."

— Bruce Lee, Bruce Lee Striking Thoughts: Bruce Lee's Wisdom for Daily Living

"Practice makes perfect. After a long time of practicing, our work will become natural, skillful, swift, and steady."

— Bruce Lee

"In Life There are No Limits, Only Plateaus."

— Bruce Lee

"Give up thinking as though not giving it up. Observe techniques as though not observing."

— Bruce Lee, Tao of Jeet Kune Do

"It is not a shame to be knocked down by other people. The important thing is to ask when you're being knocked down, 'Why am I being knocked down?' If a person can reflect in this way, then there is hope for this person."

— Bruce Lee

"Do not allow negative thoughts to enter your mind for they are the weeds that strange confidence."

— Bruce Lee

"Put 'going the extra mile' to work
as part of one's daily habit."

— Bruce Lee

"What you must not do now is to worry and think of the Nationals that is now of the past. What you HABITUALLY THINK largely determines what you will become. Remember, success is a journey, not a destination. I have faith in your ability. You will do just fine."

— Bruce Lee, Letters of the Dragon

"The attitude, "You can win if you want to badly enough," means that the will to win is constant. No amount of punishment, no amount of effort, no condition is too "tough" to take in order to win. Such an attitude can be developed only if winning is closely tied to the practitioner's ideals and dreams."

— Bruce Lee, Tao of Jeet Kune Do

"Jeet Kune Do, you see, has no definite lines or boundaries — only those you make yourself."

— Bruce Lee, Tao of Jeet Kune Do

"We have great work ahead of us, and it needs devotion and much, much energy. To grow, to discover, we need involvement, which is something I experience every day — sometimes good, sometimes frustrating. No matter what, you must let your inner light guide you out of the darkness."

— Bruce Lee

"I wish neither to possess nor to be possessed. I no longer covet 'paradise'. More important, I no longer fear 'hell'.

The medicine for my suffering I had within me from the very beginning but I did not take it. My ailment came from within myself, but I did not observe it, until this moment.

Now I see that I will never find the light unless, like the candle, I am my own fuel, consuming myself."

— Bruce Lee

"The ideal is unnatural naturalness, or natural unnaturalness. I mean it is a combination of both.

I mean here is natural instinct and here is control. You are to combine the two in harmony.

Not if you have one to the extreme, you'll be very unscientific.

If you have another to the extreme, you become, all of a sudden, a mechanical man

No longer a human being.

It is a successful combination of both.

That way it is a process of continuing growth.

Be water, my friend."

— **Bruce Lee, Bruce Lee: Artist of Life**

"My style? You can call it the art of fighting without fighting."

— Bruce Lee

"Never trouble trouble till trouble troubles you. I'll not willingly offend, nor be easily offended."

— Bruce Lee

"The martial arts are based upon understanding, hard work and a total comprehension of skills. Power training and the use of force are easy, but total comprehension of all of the skills of the martial arts is very difficult to achieve."

— Bruce Lee, Tao of Jeet Kune Do: New Expanded Edition

"To understand techniques, you must learn that they contain a lot of condensed movement."

— Bruce Lee, Tao of Jeet Kune Do: New Expanded Edition

Bruce Lee Biography

http://www.brucelee.com/bruceleec
om/file/biography.pdf